Write It Right

A LITTLE BLACKLIST OF LITERARY FAULTS

Ambrose Bierce

With a New Introduction by
Paul Dickson

DOVER PUBLICATIONS, INC.
Mineola, New York

Bibliographical Note

Write It Right: A Little Blacklist of Literary Faults, first published
by Dover Publications, Inc., in 2010, is an unabridged republication
of the work originally published by the Neale Publishing Company,
New York, in 1909.

Library of Congress Cataloging-in-Publication Data

Bierce, Ambrose, 1842–1914?
    Write it right : a little blacklist of literary faults / Ambrose Bierce ;
with a new introduction by Paul Dickson.
    p. cm.
  ISBN-13: 978-0-486-47310-9
  ISBN-10: 0-486-47310-4
    1. English language—Errors of usage.   I. Title.
PE1460.B5 2010
428—dc22

                                                                2009042828

Manufactured in the United States by Courier Corporation
47310401
www.doverpublications.com

Introduction to the Dover Edition

Write It Right: A Little Blacklist of Literary Faults was first published in 1909. Based on the premise that "good writing is clear thinking made visible," and designed to teach precision by examples in which "Narrow etymons of the mere scholar and loose locutions of the ignorant are alike denied a standing," this minutely prescriptive, formal handbook of usage was an immediate sensation. It still has a following today among those who choose, even in the e-mail age, to follow very tight rules of usage and observe a lexical purity that, for instance, eschews the word *dilapidate* when applied to anything but a crumbling stone structure because part of the Latin root of the word is *lapis* (stone).

The book is not only important as a lesson in how language usage has evolved since Ambrose Bierce's day, but it also serves as a key to the personality and precise, caustic writing style of a man many regard as one of our finest writers. Paul Fatout wrote, in his 1951 Bierce biography, *The Devil's Lexicographer,* that *Write It Right* is an extension of the man himself: "Since he was crotchety about precision, his best prose has a chiseled austerity suited to the character of a man who could never feel close to others; the reader, while admiring exactitude, may feel that he is being kept at a distance by avoidance of the informal and earthy."

In terms of *Write It Right* being a style manual, there are points here that are still altogether valid—he blacklists all modifiers for *unique* ("there are no degrees of uniqueness"), proclaims that the word *literally* is overused, and so forth—but there are many, many prohibitions we take for granted today as perfectly acceptable. For instance, Bierce would forbid us from saying or writing a *coat of paint* (*coating* was correct), or *spending time.* " 'Spend' denotes a voluntary relinquishment, but time goes from us against our will," he notes, and he brands *tantamount* as an "illegitimate and ludicrous" word.

Write It Right reflects, to some extent, a time in American history when the descriptive lexicography of Noah Webster was challenging the prescriptive King's English, and writers such as Gelett Burgess and George Ade were experimenting with language in the wake of Mark Twain's great impact as a truly American voice.

Bierce was fiercely anti-slang. "Slang is the speech of him who robs the literary garbage cans on their way to the dumps" is the line from Ambrose Bierce that H. L. Mencken quotes to set up the section on slang in his monumental *The American Language,* first published in 1921. That which Bierce castigates—slang, American idioms—Mencken celebrates.

Even the notion of an "American language" would have offended Bierce, who displays an Anglocentric disdain for sturdy, time-tested Americanisms such *as bogus, climb down, fetch, hail from, over with, likely, settle the bill, later on,* and *to side with*—all of which are forbidden in *Write It Right.* "He had a well-tuned ear for the American vernacular, it seems," wrote columnist Jan Freeman in the *Boston Globe* in 2005, "but he didn't much like what he heard."

The battle here is precision versus clarity; purity versus vernacular. Bierce argues that if one is hit "over the head" by a criminal, then the blow has missed. This is precisely correct, as one could and many would still argue, but it is also a degree less clear to those who have grown up with the idiom of "being hit over the head."

"A volume that should be in the vest pocket of every writer," proclaimed the original 1909 advertising copy for *Write It Right* (odds are that Bierce never approved the ad copy because, in the book being advertised, he opposed the word *vest,* preferring instead the British *waistcoat*). Paul Fatout commented that Bierce was so much the purist that, even in personal letters, he enclosed in quotes those native expressions that he considered unacceptable: *whole lot, draw the line, drop in,* and so on.

Robert L. Gale, in *The Ambrose Bierce Companion,* termed *Write It Right* "ultraconservative" in its position on grammar and semantics and said that its "rigid, austere stance" is hard to square with the implications of the definition of "lexicographer" in Bierce's *Devil's Dictionary*—which refers to the "bold and discerning writer . . . recognizing the truth that language must grow by innovation if it grow at all, makes new words and uses the old in an unfamiliar sense"—a seeming contradiction that just adds to the mystery of a man who disappeared into the Mexican countryside a few years after *Write It Right* was published.

—Paul Dickson

AIMS AND THE PLAN

The author's main purpose in this book is to teach precision in writing; and of good writing (which, essentially, is clear thinking made visible) precision is the point of capital concern. It is attained by choice of the word that accurately and adequately expresses what the writer has in mind, and by exclusion of that which either denotes or connotes something else. As Quintilian puts it, the writer should so write that his reader not only may, but must, understand.

Few words have more than one literal and serviceable meaning, however many metaphorical, derivative, related, or even unrelated, meanings lexicographers may think it worth while to gather from all sorts and conditions of men, with which to bloat their absurd and misleading dictionaries. This actual and serviceable meaning—not always determined by derivation, and seldom by popular usage—is the one affirmed, according to his light, by the author of this little manual of solecisms. Narrow etymons of the mere scholar and loose locutions of the ignorant are alike denied a standing.

1

The plan of the book is more illustrative than expository, the aim being to use the terms of etymology and syntax as little as is compatible with clarity, familiar example being more easily apprehended than technical precept. When both are employed the precept is commonly given after the example has prepared the student to apply it, not only to the matter in mind, but to similar matters not mentioned. Everything in quotation marks is to be understood as disapproved.

Not all locutions blacklisted herein are always to be reprobated as universal outlaws. Excepting in the case of capital offenders—expressions ancestrally vulgar or irreclaimably degenerate—absolute proscription is possible as to serious composition only; in other forms the writer must rely on his sense of values and the fitness of things. While it is true that some colloquialisms and, with less of license, even some slang, may be sparingly employed in light literature, for point, piquancy or any of the purposes of the skilled writer sensible to the necessity and charm of keeping at least one foot on the ground, to others the virtue of restraint may be commended as distinctly superior to the joy of indulgence.

Precision is much, but not all; some words and

phrases are disallowed on the ground of taste. As there are neither standards nor arbiters of taste, the book can do little more than reflect that of its author, who is far indeed from professing impeccability. In neither taste nor precision is any man's practice a court of last appeal, for writers all, both great and small, are habitual sinners against the light; and their accuser is cheerfully aware that his own work will supply (as in making this book it has supplied) many "awful examples"—his later work less abundantly, he hopes, than his earlier. He nevertheless believes that this does not disqualify him for showing by other instances than his own how not to write. The infallible teacher is still in the forest primeval, throwing seeds to the white blackbirds.

A. B.

THE BLACKLIST

A for *An*. "A hotel." "A heroic man." Before an unaccented aspirate use an. The contrary usage in this country comes of too strongly stressing our aspirates.

Action for *Act*. "In wrestling, a blow is a reprehensible action." A blow is not an action but an act. An action may consist of many acts.

Admission for *Admittance*. "The price of admission is one dollar."

Admit for *Confess*. To admit is to concede something affirmed. An unaccused offender cannot admit his guilt.

Adopt. "He adopted a disguise." One may adopt a child, or an opinion, but a disguise is assumed.

Advisedly for *Advertently, Intentionally*. "It was done advisedly" should mean that it was done after advice.

Afford. It is not well to say "the fact affords a reasonable presumption"; "the house afforded ample accommodation." The fact supplies a reasonable presumption. The house offered, or gave, ample accommodation.

Afraid. Do not say, "I am afraid it will rain." Say, I fear that it will rain.

Afterwards for *Afterward.*

Aggravate for *Irritate.* "He aggravated me by his insolence." To aggravate is to augment the disagreeableness of something already disagreeable, or the badness of something bad. But a person cannot be aggravated, even if disagreeable or bad. Women are singularly prone to misuse of this word.

All of. "He gave all of his property." The words are contradictory: an entire thing cannot be of itself. Omit the preposition.

Alleged. "The alleged murderer." One can allege a murder, but not a murderer; a crime, but not a criminal. A man that is merely suspected of crime would not, in any case, be an alleged criminal, for an allegation is a definite and positive statement. In their tiresome addiction to this use of alleged, the newspapers, though having mainly in mind the danger of libel suits, can urge in further justification the lack of any other single word that exactly expresses their meaning; but the fact that a mud-puddle supplies the shortest route is not a compelling reason for walking through it. One can go around.

Allow for *Permit.* "I allow you to go." Precision is better attained by saying permit, for allow has other meanings.

Allude to for *Mention.* What is alluded to is not mentioned, but referred to indirectly. Originally, the word implied a playful, or sportive, reference. That meaning is gone out of it.

And so. And yet. "And so they were married." "And yet a woman." Omit the conjunction.

And which. And who. These forms are incorrect unless the relative pronoun has been used previously in the sentence. "The colt, spirited and strong, and which was unbroken, escaped from the pasture." "John Smith, one of our leading merchants, and who fell from a window yesterday, died this morning." Omit the conjunction.

Antecedents for *Personal History.* Antecedents are predecessors.

Anticipate for *Expect.* "I anticipate trouble." To anticipate is to act on an expectation in a way to promote or forestall the event expected.

Anxious for *Eager.* "I was anxious to go." Anxious should not be followed by an infinitive. Anxiety is contemplative; eagerness, alert for action.

Appreciate for *Highly Value.* In the sense of value, it means value justly, not highly. In another and preferable sense it means to increase in value.

Approach. "The juror was approached"; that is, overtures were made to him with a view to bribing him. As there is no other single word for it, approach is made to serve, figuratively; and being graphic, it is not altogether objectionable.

Appropriated for *Took.* "He appropriated his neighbor's horse to his own use." To appropriate is to set apart, as a sum of money, for a special purpose.

Approve of for *Approve.* There is no sense in making approve an intransitive verb.

Apt for *Likely.* "One is apt to be mistaken." Apt means facile, felicitous, ready, and the like; but even the dictionary-makers cannot persuade a person of discriminating taste to accept it as synonymous with likely.

Around for *About.* "The débris of battle lay around them." "The huckster went around, crying his wares." Around carries the concept of circularity.

Article. A good and useful word, but used without meaning by shopkeepers; as, "A good article of vinegar," for a good vinegar.

As for *That*, or *If*. "I do not know as he is living." This error is not very common among those who can write at all, but one sometimes sees it in high place.

As—as for *So—as*. "He is not as good as she." Say, not so good. In affirmative sentences the rule is different: He is as good as she.

As for for *As to*. "As for me, I am well." Say, as to me.

At Auction for *by Auction*. "The goods were sold at auction."

At for *By*. "She was shocked at his conduct." This very common solecism is without excuse.

Attain for *Accomplish*. "By diligence we attain our purpose." A purpose is accomplished; success is attained.

Authoress. A needless word—as needless as "poetess."

Avocation for *Vocation*. A vocation is, literally, a calling; that is, a trade or profession. An avocation is something that calls one away from it. If I say that farming is some one's avocation I mean that he practises it, not regularly, but at odd times.

Avoid for *Avert.* "By displaying a light the skipper avoided a collision." To avoid is to shun; the skipper could have avoided a collision only by getting out of the way.

Avoirdupois for *Weight.* Mere slang.

*

Back of for *Behind, At the Back of.* "Back of law is force."

Backwards for *Backward.*

Badly for *Bad.* "I feel badly." "He looks badly." The former sentence implies defective nerves of sensation, the latter, imperfect vision. Use the adjective.

Balance for *Remainder.* "The balance of my time is given to recreation." In this sense balance is a commercial word, and relates to accounting.

Banquet. A good enough word in its place, but its place is the dictionary. Say, dinner.

Bar for *Bend.* "Bar sinister." There is no such thing in heraldry as a bar sinister.

Because for *For.* "I knew it was night, because it was dark." "He will not go, because he is ill."

Bet for *Betted.* The verb to bet forms its preterite regularly, as do wet, wed, knit, quit and others that are commonly misconjugated. It seems that we clip our short words more than we do our long.

Body for *Trunk.* "The body lay here, the head there." The body is the entire physical person (as distinguished from the soul, or mind) and the head is a part of it. As distinguished from head, trunk may include the limbs, but anatomically it is the torso only.

Bogus for *Counterfeit,* or *False.* The word is slang; keep it out.

Both. This word is frequently misplaced; as, "A large mob, both of men and women." Say, of both men and women.

Both alike. "They are both alike." Say, they are alike. One of them could not be alike.

Brainy. Pure slang, and singularly disagreeable.

Bug for *Beetle,* or for anything. Do not use it.

Business for *Right.* "He has no business to go there."

Build for *Make.* "Build a fire." "Build a canal." Even "build a tunnel" is not unknown, and probably if the woodchuck is skilled in the American tongue he speaks of building a hole.

But. By many writers this word (in the sense of except) is regarded as a preposition, to be followed by the objective case: "All went but him." It is not a preposition and may take either the nominative or objective case, to agree with the subject or the object of the verb. All went but he. The natives killed all but him.

But what. "I did not know but what he was an enemy." Omit *what.* If condemnation of this dreadful locution seem needless bear the matter in mind in your reading and you will soon be of a different opinion.

By for *Of.* "A man by the name of Brown." Say, of the name. Better than either form is: a man named Brown.

*

Calculated for *Likely.* "The bad weather is calculated to produce sickness." Calculated implies calculation, design.

Can for *May.* "Can I go fishing?" "He can call on me if he wishes to."

Candidate for *Aspirant.* In American politics, one is not a candidate for an office until formally named (nominated) for it by a convention, or otherwise, as provided by law or custom. So when a man who is moving Heaven and Earth to procure the nomination protests that he is "not a candidate" he tells the truth in order to deceive.

Cannot for *Can*. "I cannot but go." Say, I can but go.

Capable. "Men are capable of being flattered." Say, susceptible to flattery. "Capable of being refuted." Vulnerable to refutation. Unlike capacity, capability is not passive, but active. We are capable of doing, not of having something done to us.

Capacity for *Ability*. "A great capacity for work." Capacity is receptive; ability, potential. A sponge has capacity for water; the hand, ability to squeeze it out.

Casket for *Coffin*. A needless euphemism affected by undertakers.

Casualties for *Losses* in Battle. The essence of casualty is accident, absence of design. Death and wounds in battle are produced otherwise, are expectable and expected, and, by the enemy, intentional.

Chance for *Opportunity*. "He had a good chance to succeed."

Chin Whiskers. The whisker grows on the cheek, not the chin.

Chivalrous. The word is popularly used in the Southern States only, and commonly has reference to men's manner toward women. Archaic, stilted and fantastic.

Citizen for *Civilian*. A soldier may be a citizen, but is not a civilian.

Claim for *Affirm*. "I claim that he is elected." To claim is to assert ownership.

Clever for *Obliging*. In this sense the word was once in general use in the United States, but is now seldom heard and life here is less insupportable.

Climb down. In climbing one ascends.

Coat for *Coating*. "A coat of paint, or varnish." If we coat something we produce a coating, not a coat.

Collateral Descendant. There can be none: a "collateral descendant" is not a descendant.

Colonel, *Judge*, *Governor*, etc., for *Mister*. Give a man a title only if it belongs to him, and only while it belongs to him.

Combine for *Combination*. The word, in this sense, has something of the meaning of conspiracy, but there is no justification for it as a noun, in any sense.

Commence for *Begin*. This is not actually incorrect, but—well, it is a matter of taste.

Commencement for *Termination*. A contribution to our noble tongue by its scholastic conservators, "commencement day" being their name for the last day of the collegiate year. It is ingeniously defended on the ground that on that day those on whom degrees are bestowed commence to hold them. Lovely!

Commit Suicide. Instead of "He committed suicide," say, He killed himself, or, He took his life. For married we do not say "committed matrimony." Unfortunately most of us do say, "got married," which is almost as bad. For lack of a suitable verb we just sometimes say committed this or that, as in the instance of bigamy, for the verb to bigam is a blessing that is still in store for us.

Compare with for *Compare to*. "He had the immodesty to compare himself with Shakespeare." Nothing necessarily immodest in that.

Comparison with may be for observing a difference; comparison to affirms a similarity.

Complected. Anticipatory past participle of the verb "to complect." Let us wait for that.

Conclude for *Decide.* "I concluded to go to town." Having concluded a course of reasoning (implied) I decided to go to town. A decision is supposed to be made at the conclusion of a course of reasoning, but is not the conclusion itself. Conversely, the conclusion of a syllogism is not a decision, but an inference.

Connection. "In this connection I should like to say a word or two." In connection with this matter.

Conscious for *Aware.* "The King was conscious of the conspiracy." We are conscious of what we feel; aware of what we know.

Consent for *Assent.* "He consented to that opinion." To consent is to agree to a proposal; to assent is to agree with a proposition.

Conservative for *Moderate.* "A conservative estimate"; "a conservative forecast"; "a conservative statement," and so on. These and many other abuses of the word are of recent growth in the newspapers and "halls of legislation."

Having been found to have several meanings, conservative seems to be thought to mean everything.

Continually and *Continuously.* It seems that these words should have the same meaning, but in their use by good writers there is a difference. What is done continually is not done all the time, but continuous action is without interruption. A loquacious fellow, who nevertheless finds time to eat and sleep, is continually talking; but a great river flows continuously.

Convoy for *Escort.* "A man-of-war acted as convoy to the flotilla." The flotilla is the convoy, the man-of-war the escort.

Couple for *Two.* For two things to be a couple they must be of one general kind, and their number unimportant to the statement made of them. It would be weak to say, "He gave me only one, although he took a couple for himself." Couple expresses indifference to the exact number, as does several. That is true, even in the phrase, a married couple, for the number is carried in the adjective and needs no emphasis.

Created for *First Performed.* Stage slang. "Burbage created the part of Hamlet." What was it that its author did to it?

Critically for *Seriously.* "He has long been critically ill." A patient is critically ill only at the crisis of his disease.

Criticise for *Condemn*, or *Disparage.* Criticism is not necessarily censorious; it may approve.

Cunning for *Amusing.* Usually said of a child, or pet. This is pure Americanese, as is its synonym, "cute."

Curious for *Odd*, or *Singular.* To be curious is to have an inquiring mind, or mood—curiosity.

Custom for *Habit.* Communities have customs; individuals, habits—commonly bad ones.

*

Decease for *Die.*

Decidedly for *Very*, or *Certainly.* "It is decidedly cold."

Declared for *Said.* To a newspaper reporter no one seems ever to say anything; all "declare." Like "alleged" (which see) the word is tiresome exceedingly.

Defalcation for *Default.* A defalcation is a cutting off, a subtraction; a default is a failure in duty.

Definitely for *Definitively*. "It was definitely decided." Definitely means precisely, with exactness; definitively means finally, conclusively.

Deliver. "He delivered an oration," or "delivered a lecture." Say, He made an oration, or gave a lecture.

Demean for *Debase* or *Degrade*. "He demeaned himself by accepting charity." The word relates, not to meanness, but to demeanor, conduct, behavior. One may demean oneself with dignity and credit.

Demise for *Death*. Usually said of a person of note. Demise means the lapse, as by death, of some authority, distinction or privilege, which passes to another than the one that held it; as the demise of the Crown.

Democracy for *Democratic Party*. One could as properly call the Christian Church "the Christianity."

Dépôt for *Station*. "Railroad dépôt." A dépôt is a place of deposit; as, a dépôt of supply for an army.

Deprivation for *Privation*. "The mendicant showed the effects of deprivation." Deprivation refers to the act of depriving, taking away from; privation is the state of destitution, of not having.

Dilapidated for *Ruined*. Said of a building, or other structure. But the word is from the Latin *lapis*, a stone, and cannot properly be used of any but a stone structure.

Directly for *Immediately*. "I will come directly" means that I will come by the most direct route.

Dirt for *Earth*, *Soil*, or *Gravel*. A most disagreeable Americanism, discredited by general (and Presidential) use. "Make the dirt fly." Dirt means filth.

Distinctly for *Distinctively*. "The custom is distinctly Oriental." Distinctly is plainly; distinctively, in a way to distinguish one thing from others.

Donate for *Give*. Good American, but not good English.

Doubtlessly. A doubly adverbial form, like "illy."

Dress for *Gown*. Not so common as it was a few years ago. Dress means the entire costume.

*

Each Other for *One Another*. "The three looked at each other." That is, each looked at the other. But there were more than one other; so we should say they looked at one another, which means that each looked at another. Of two, say each other; of more than two, one another.

Edify for *Please*, or *Entertain*. Edify means to build; it has, therefore, the sense of uplift, improvement—usually moral, or spiritual.

Electrocution. To one having even an elementary knowledge of Latin grammar this word is no less than disgusting, and the thing meant by it is felt to be altogether too good for the word's inventor.

Empty for *Vacant*. Say, an empty bottle; but, a vacant house.

Employé. Good French, but bad English. Say, employee.

Endorse for *Approve*. To endorse is to write upon the back of, or to sign the promissory note of another. It is a commercial word, having insufficient dignity for literary use. You may endorse a check, but you approve a policy, or statement.

Endways. A corruption of endwise.

Entitled for *Authorized, Privileged*. "The man is not entitled to draw rations." Say, entitled to rations. Entitled is not to be followed by an infinitive.

Episode for *Occurrence, Event*, etc. Properly, an episode is a narrative that is a subordinate part of another narrative. An occurrence considered by itself is not an episode.

Equally as for *Equally.* "This is equally as good." Omit as. "He was of the same age, and equally as tall." Say, equally tall.

Equivalent for *Equal.* "My salary is equivalent to yours."

Essential for *Necessary.* This solecism is common among the best writers of this country and England. "It is essential to go early"; "Irrigation is essential to cultivation of arid lands," and so forth. One thing is essential to another thing only if it is of the essence of it—an important and indispensable part of it, determining its nature; the soul of it.

Even for *Exact.* "An even dozen."

Every for *Entire, Full.* "The president had every confidence in him."

Every for *Ever.* "Every now and then." This is nonsense: there can be no such thing as a now and then, nor, of course, a number of now and thens. Now and then is itself bad enough, reversing as it does the sequence of things, but it is idiomatic and there is no quarreling with it. But "every" is here a corruption of ever, meaning repeatedly, continually.

Ex. "Ex-President," "an ex-convict," and the like. Say, former. In England one may say, Mr. Roosevelt, sometime President; though the usage is a trifle archaic.

Example for *Problem.* A heritage from the text-books. "An example in arithmetic." An equally bad word for the same thing is "sum": "Do the sum," for Solve the problem.

Excessively for *Exceedingly.* "The disease is excessively painful." "The weather is excessively cold." Anything that is painful at all is excessively so. Even a slight degree or small amount of what is disagreeable or injurious is excessive—that is to say, redundant, superfluous, not required.

Executed. "The condemned man was executed." He was hanged, or otherwise put to death; it is the sentence that is executed.

Executive for *Secret.* An executive session of a deliberative body is a session for executive business, as distinguished from legislative. It is commonly secret, but a secret session is not necessarily executive.

Expect for *Believe*, or *Suppose*. "I expect he will go." Say, I believe (suppose or think) he will go; or, I expect him to go.

Expectorate for *Spit*. The former word is frequently used, even in laws and ordinances, as a euphemism for the latter. It not only means something entirely different, but to one with a Latin ear is far more offensive.

Experience for *Suffer*, or *Undergo*. "The sinner experienced a change of heart." This will do if said lightly or mockingly. It does not indicate a serious frame of mind in the speaker.

Extend for *Proffer*. "He extended an invitation." One does not always hold out an invitation in one's hand; it may be spoken or sent.

*

Fail. "He failed to note the hour." That implies that he tried to note it, but did not succeed. Failure carries always the sense of endeavor; when there has been no endeavor there is no failure. A falling stone cannot fail to strike you, for it does not try; but a marksman firing at you may fail to hit you; and I hope he always will.

Favor for *Resemble*. "The child favors its father."

Feel of for *Feel.* "The doctor felt of the patient's head." "Smell of" and "taste of" are incorrect too.

Feminine for *Female.* "A feminine member of the club." Feminine refers, not to sex proper, but to gender, which may be defined as the sex of words. The same is true of masculine.

Fetch for *Bring.* Fetching includes, not only bringing, but going to get—going for and returning with. You may bring what you did not go for.

Finances for *Wealth*, or *Pecuniary Resources.*

Financial for *Pecuniary.* "His financial reward"; "he is financially responsible," and so forth.

Firstly. If this word could mean anything it would mean firstlike, whatever that might mean. The ordinal numbers should have no adverbial form: "firstly," "secondly," and the rest are words without meaning.

Fix. This is, in America, a word-of-all-work, most frequently meaning repair, or prepare. Do not so use it.

Forebears for *Ancestors.* The word is ometimes spelled forbears, a worse spelling than the other, but not much. If used at all it should be spelled *forebeers*, for it means those who have *been* before. A forebe-er is one who fore-was. Considered in any way, it is a senseless word.

Forecasted. For this abominable word we are indebted to the weather bureau—at least it was not sent upon us until that affliction was with us. Let us hope that it may some day be losted from the language.

Former and *Latter.* Indicating the first and the second of things previously named, these words are unobjectionable if not too far removed from the names that they stand for. If they are they confuse, for the reader has to look back to the names. Use them sparingly.

Funeral Obsequies. Tautological. Say, obsequies; the word is now used in none but a funereal sense.

Fully for *Definitively*, or *Finally*. "After many preliminary examinations he was fully committed for trial." The adverb is meaningless: a defendant is never partly committed for trial. This is a solecism to which lawyers are addicted. And sometimes they have been heard to say "fullied."

Funds for *Money*. "He was out of funds." Funds are not money in general, but sums of money or credit available for particular purposes.

Furnish for *Provide*, or *Supply*. "Taxation furnished the money." A pauper may furnish a house if some one will provide the furniture, or the money to buy it. "His flight furnishes a presumption of guilt." It supplies it.

*

Generally for *Usually*. "The winds are generally high." "A fool is generally vain." This misuse of the word appears to come of abbreviating: Generally speaking, the weather is bad. A fool, to speak generally, is vain.

Gent for *Gentleman*. Vulgar exceedingly.

Genteel. This word, meaning polite, or well mannered, was once in better repute than it is now, and its noun, gentility, is still not infrequently found in the work of good writers. Genteel is most often used by those who write, as the Scotchman of the anecdote joked—wi' deeficulty.

Gentleman. It is not possible to teach the correct use of this overworked word: one must be bred to it. Everybody knows that it is not synonymous with man, but among the "genteel" and those ambitious to be thought "genteel" it is commonly so used in discourse too formal for the word "gent." To use the word gentleman correctly, be one.

Genuine for *Authentic*, or *Veritable.* "A genuine document," "a genuine surprise," and the like.

Given. "The soldier was given a rifle." What was given is the rifle, not the soldier. "The house was given a coat (coating) of paint." Nothing can be "given" anything.

Goatee. In this country goatee is frequently used for a tuft of beard on the point of the chin—what is sometimes called "an imperial," apparently because the late Emperor Napoleon III wore his beard so. His Majesty the Goat is graciously pleased to wear his beneath the chin.

Got Married for *Married.* If this is correct we should say, also, "got dead" for died; one expression is as good as the other.

Gotten for *Got.* This has gone out of good use, though in such compounded words as begotten and misbegotten it persists respectably.

Graduated for *Was Graduated.*

Gratuitous for *Unwarranted.* "A gratuitous assertion." Gratuitous means without cost.

Grueling. Used chiefly by newspaper reporters; as, "He was subjected to a grueling cross-examination." "It was grueling weather." Probably a corruption of grilling.

Gubernatorial. Eschew it; it is not English, is needless and bombastic. Leave it to those who call a political office a "chair." "Gubernatorial chair" is good enough for them. So is hanging.

*

Had Better for *Would Better.* This is not defensible as an idiom, as those who always used it before their attention was directed to it take the trouble to point out. It comes of such contractions as he'd for he would, I'd for I would. These clipped words are erroneously restored as "he had," "I had." So we have such monstrosities as "He had better beware," "I had better go."

Hail for *Come.* "He hails from Chicago." This is sea speech, and comes from the custom of hailing passing ships. It will not do for serious discourse.

Have Got for *Have.* "I have got a good horse" directs attention rather to the act of getting than to the state of having, and represents the capture as recently completed.

Head over Heels. A transposition of words hardly less surprising than (to the person most concerned) the mischance that it fails to describe. What is meant is heels over head.

Healthy for *Wholesome.* "A healthy climate." "A healthy occupation." Only a living thing can be healthy.

Helpmeet for *Helpmate.* In Genesis Adam's wife is called "an help meet for him," that is, fit for him. The ridiculous word appears to have had no other origin.

Hereafter for *Henceforth.* Hereafter means at some time in the future; henceforth, always in the future. The penitent who promises to be good hereafter commits himself to the performance of a single good act, not to a course of good conduct.

Honeymoon. Moon here means month, so it is incorrect to say, "a week's honeymoon," or, "Their honeymoon lasted a year."

Horseflesh for *Horses.* A singularly senseless and disagreeable word which, when used, as it commonly is, with reference to hippophilism, savors rather more of the spit than of the spirit.

Humans as a Noun. We have no single word having the general yet limited meaning that this is sometimes used to express—a meaning corresponding to that of the word animals, as the word men would if it included women and children. But there is time enough to use two words.

Hung for *Hanged.* A bell, or a curtain, is hung, but a man is hanged. Hung is the junior form of the participle, and is now used for everything but man. Perhaps it is our reverence for the custom of hanging men that sacredly preserves the elder form—as some, even, of the most zealous American spelling reformers still respect the u in Saviour.

Hurry for *Haste* and *Hasten.* To hurry is to hasten in a more or less disorderly manner. Hurry is misused, also, in another sense: "There is no hurry"—meaning, There is no reason for haste.

Hurt for *Harm.* "It does no hurt." To be hurt is to feel pain, but one may be harmed without knowing it. To spank a child, or flout a fool, hurts without harming.

*

Idea for *Thought, Purpose, Expectation*, etc. "I had no idea that it was so cold." "When he went abroad it was with no idea of remaining."

Identified with. "He is closely identified with the temperance movement." Say, connected.

Ilk for *Kind.* "Men of that ilk." This Scotch word has a narrowly limited and specific meaning. It relates to an ancestral estate having the same name as the person spoken of. Macdonald of that ilk means, Macdonald of Macdonald. The phrase quoted above is without meaning.

Illy for *Ill.* There is no such word as illy, for ill itself is an adverb.

Imaginary Line. The adjective is needless. Geometrically, every line is imaginary; its graphic representation is a mark. True the text-books say, draw a line, but in a mathematical sense the line already exists; the drawing only makes its course visible.

In for *Into.* "He was put in jail." "He went in the house." A man may be in jail, or be in a house, but when the act of entrance—the movement of something from the outside to the inside of another thing—is related the correct word is into if the latter thing is named.

Inaugurate for *Begin*, *Establish*, etc. Inauguration implies some degree of formality and ceremony.

Incumbent for *Obligatory*. "It was incumbent upon me to relieve him." Infelicitous and work-worn. Say, It was my duty, or, if enamored of that particular metaphor, It lay upon me.

Individual. As a noun, this word means something that cannot be considered as divided, a unit. But it is incorrect to call a man, woman or child an individual, except with reference to mankind, to society or to a class of persons. It will not do to say, "An individual stood in the street," when no mention nor allusion has been made, nor is going to be made, to some aggregate of individuals considered as a whole.

Indorse. See *Endorse*.

Insane Asylum. Obviously an asylum cannot be unsound in mind. Say, asylum for the insane.

In Spite of. In most instances it is better to say despite.

Inside of. Omit the preposition.

Insignificant for *Trivial*, or *Small*. Insignificant means not signifying anything, and should be used only in contrast, expressed or implied, with something that is important for what it implies. The bear's tail may be insignificant to a naturalist tracing the animal's descent from an earlier species, but to the rest of us, not concerned with the matter, it is merely small.

Insoluble for *Unsolvable.* Use the former word for material substances, the latter for problems.

Inst., Prox., Ult. These abbreviations of *instante mense* (in the present month), *proximo mense* (in the next month) and *ultimo mense* (in the last month), are serviceable enough in commercial correspondence, but, like A.M., P.M. and many other contractions of Latin words, could profitably be spared from literature.

Integrity for *Honesty.* The word means entireness, wholeness. It may be rightly used to affirm possession of all the virtues, that is, unity of moral character.

Involve for *Entail.* "Proof of the charges will involve his dismissal." Not at all; it will entail it. To involve is, literally, to infold, not to bring about, nor cause to ensue. An unofficial investigation, for example, may involve character and reputation, but the ultimate consequence is entailed. A question, in the parliamentary sense, may involve a principle; its settlement one way or another may entail expense, or injury to interests. An act may involve one's honor and entail disgrace.

It for *So*. "Going into the lion's cage is dangerous; you should not do it." Do so is the better expression, as a rule, for the word it is a pronoun, meaning a thing, or object, and therefore incapable of being done. Colloquially we may say do it, or do this, or do that, but in serious written discourse greater precision is desirable, and is better obtained, in most cases, by use of the adverb.

Item for *Brief Article*. Commonly used of a narrative in a newspaper. Item connotes an aggregate of which it is a unit—one thing of many. Hence it suggests more than we may wish to direct attention to.

*

Jackies for *Sailors*. Vulgar, and especially offensive to seamen.

Jeopardize for *Imperil*, or *Endanger*. The correct word is jeopard, but in any case there is no need for anything so farfetched and stilted.

Juncture. Juncture means a joining, a junction; its use to signify a time, however critical a time, is absurd. "At this juncture the woman screamed." In reading that account of it we scream too.

Just Exactly. Nothing is gained in strength nor precision by this kind of pleonasm. Omit just.

Juvenile for *Child*. This needless use of the adjective for the noun is probably supposed to be humorous, like "canine" for dog, "optic" for eye, "anatomy" for body, and the like. Happily the offense is not very common.

*

Kind of a for *Kind of*. "He was that kind of a man." Say that kind of man. Man here is generic, and a genus comprises many kinds. But there cannot be more than one kind of one thing. *Kind of* followed by an adjective, as, "kind of good," is almost too gross for censure.

*

Landed Estate for *Property in Land*. Dreadful!

Last and *Past*. "Last week." "The past week." Neither is accurate: a week cannot be the last if another is already begun; and all weeks except this one are past. Here two wrongs seem to make a right: we can say the week last past. But will we? I trow not.

Later on. On is redundant; say, later.

Laundry. Meaning a place where clothing is washed, this word cannot mean, also, clothing sent there to be washed.

Lay (to place) for *Lie* (to recline). "The ship lays on her side." A more common error is made in the past tense, as, "He laid down on the grass." The confusion comes of the identity of a present tense of the transitive verb to lay and the past tense of the intransitive verb to lie.

Leading Question. A leading question is not necessarily an important one; it is one that is so framed as to suggest, or lead to, the answer desired. Few others than lawyers use the term correctly.

Lease. To say of a man that he leases certain premises leaves it doubtful whether he is lessor or lessee. Being ambiguous, the word should be used with caution.

Leave for *Go away.* "He left yesterday." Leave is a transitive verb; name the place of departure.

Leave for *Let.* "Leave it alone." By this many persons mean, not that it is to be left in solitude, but that it is to be untouched, or unmolested.

Lengthways for *Lengthwise.*

Lengthy. Usually said in disparagement of some wearisome discourse. It is no better than breadthy, or thicknessy.

Leniency for *Lenity.* The words are synonymous, but the latter is the better.

Less for *Fewer.* "The regiment had less than five hundred men." Less relates to quantity, fewer, to number.

Limited for *Small, Inadequate,* etc. "The army's operations were confined to a limited area." "We had a limited supply of food." A large area and an adequate supply would also be limited. Everything that we know about is limited.

Liable for *Likely.* "Man is liable to err." Man is not liable to err, but to error. Liable should be followed, not by an infinitive, but by a preposition.

Like for *As,* or *As if.* "The matter is now like it was." "The house looked like it would fall."

Likely for *Probably.* "He will likely be elected." If likely is thought the better word (and in most cases it is) put it this way: "It is likely that he will be elected," or, "He is likely to be elected."

Line for *Kind*, or *Class*. "This line of goods." Leave the word to "salesladies" and "salesgentlemen." "That line of business." Say, that business.

Literally for *Figuratively*. "The stream was literally alive with fish." "His eloquence literally swept the audience from its feet." It is bad enough to exaggerate, but to affirm the truth of the exaggeration is intolerable.

Loan for *Lend*. "I loaned him ten dollars." We lend, but the act of lending, or, less literally, the thing lent, is a loan.

Locate. "After many removals the family located at Smithville." Some dictionaries give locate as an intransitive verb having that meaning, but— well, dictionaries are funny.

Lots, or *a Lot*, for *Much*, or *Many*. "Lots of things." "A lot of talk."

Love for *Like*. "I love to travel." "I love apples." Keep the stronger word for a stronger feeling.

Lunch for *Luncheon*. But do not use luncheon as a verb.

*

Mad for *Angry*. An Americanism of lessening prevalence. It is probable that anger is a kind of madness (insanity), but that is not what the misusers of the word mad mean to affirm.

Maintain for *Contend.* "The senator maintained that the tariff was iniquitous." He maintained it only if he proved it.

Majority for *Plurality.* Concerning votes cast in an election, a majority is more than half the total; a plurality is the excess of one candidate's votes over another's. Commonly the votes compared are those for the successful candidate and those for his most nearly successful competitor.

Make for *Earn.* "He makes fifty dollars a month by manual labor."

Mansion for *Dwelling,* or *House.* Usually mere hyperbole, a lamentable fault of our national literature. Even our presidents, before Roosevelt, called their dwelling the Executive Mansion.

Masculine for *Male.* See *Feminine.*

Mend for *Repair.* "They mended the road." To mend is to repair, but to repair is not always to mend. A stocking is mended, a road repaired.

Meet for *Meeting.* This belongs to the language of sport, which persons of sense do not write—nor read.

Militate. "Negligence militates against success." If "militate" meant anything it would mean fight, but there is no such word.

Mind for *Obey.* This is a reasonless extension of one legitimate meaning of mind, namely, to heed, to give attention.

Minus for *Lacking*, or *Without*. "After the battle he was minus an ear." It is better in serious composition to avoid such alien words as have vernacular equivalents.

Mistaken for *Mistake.* "You are mistaken." For whom? Say, You mistake.

Monarch for *King, Emperor*, or *Sovereign*. Not only hyperbolical, but inaccurate. There is not a monarch in Christendom.

Moneyed for *Wealthy.* "The moneyed men of New York." One might as sensibly say, "The cattled men of Texas," or, "The lobstered men of the fish market."

Most for *Almost.* "The apples are most all gone." "The returning travelers were most home."

Moved for *Removed.* "The family has moved to another house." "The Joneses were moving."

Mutual. By this word we express a reciprocal relation. It implies exchange, a giving and taking, not a mere possessing in common. There can be a mutual affection, or a mutual hatred, but not a mutual friend, nor a mutual horse.

*

Name for *Title and Name.* "His name was Mr. Smith." Surely no babe was ever christened Mister.

Necessaries for *Means.* "Bread and meat are necessaries of life." Not so; they are the mere means, for one can, and many do, live comfortably without them. Food and drink are necessaries of life, but particular kinds of food and drink are not.

Necessities for *Necessaries.* "Necessities of life are those things without which we cannot live."

Née. Feminine of *né*, born. "Mrs. Jones, *née* Lucy Smith." She could hardly have been christened before her birth. If you must use the French word say, *née* Smith.

Negotiate. From the Latin *negotium*. It means, as all know, to fix the terms for a transaction, to bargain. But when we say, "The driver negotiated a difficult turn of the road," or, "The chauffeur negotiated a hill," we speak nonsense.

Neither—or for *Neither—nor.* "Neither a cat or fish has wool." Always after neither use nor.

New Beginner for *Beginner.*

Nice for *Good,* or *Agreeable.* "A nice girl." Nice means fastidious, delicately discriminative, and the like. Pope uses the word admirably of a dandy who was skilled in the nice conduct [management] of a clouded cane.

Noise for *Sound.* "A noise like a flute"; "a noise of twittering birds," etc. A noise is a loud or disagreeable sound, or combination or succession of sounds.

None. Usually, and in most cases, singular; as, None has come. But it is not singular because it always means not one, for frequently it does not, as, The bottle was full of milk, but none is left. When it refers to numbers, not quantity, popular usage stubbornly insists that it is plural, and at least one respectable authority says that as a singular it is offensive. One is sorry to be offensive to a good man.

No Use. "He tried to smile, but it was no use." Say, of no use, or, less colloquially, in vain.

Novel for *Romance.* In a novel there is at least an apparent attention to considerations of probability; it is a narrative of what might occur. Romance flies with a free wing and owns no allegiance to likelihood. Both are fiction, both works of imagination, but should not be confounded. They are as distinct as beast and bird.

Numerous for *Many*. Rightly used, numerous relates to numbers, but does not imply a great number. A correct use is seen in the term numerous verse—verse consisting of poetic numbers; that is, rhythmical feet.

*

Obnoxious for *Offensive*. Obnoxious means exposed to evil. A soldier in battle is obnoxious to danger.

Occasion for *Induce*, or *Cause*. "His arrival occasioned a great tumult." As a verb, the word is needless and unpleasing.

Occasional Poems. These are not, as so many authors and compilers seem to think, poems written at irregular and indefinite intervals, but poems written for *occasions*, such as anniversaries, festivals, celebrations and the like.

Of Any for *Of All*. "The greatest poet of any that we have had."

Offhanded and *Offhandedly*. Offhand is both adjective and adverb; these are bastard forms.

On the Street. A street comprises the roadway and the buildings at each side. Say, in the street. He lives in Broadway.

One Another for *Each Other*. See *Each Other*.

Only. "He only had one." Say, He had only one, or, better, one only. The other sentence might be taken to mean that only he had one; that, indeed, is what it distinctly says. The correct placing of only in a sentence requires attention and skill.

Opine for *Think*. The word is not very respectably connected.

Opposite for *Contrary*. "I hold the opposite opinion." "The opposite practice."

Or for *Nor*. Probably our most nearly universal solecism. "I cannot see the sun or the moon." This means that I am unable to see one of them, though I may see the other. By using nor, I affirm the invisibility of both, which is what I wanted to do. If a man is not white or black he may nevertheless be a Negro or a Caucasian; but if he is not white nor black he belongs to some other race. See *Neither*.

Ordinarily for *Usually*. Clumsy.

Ovation. In ancient Rome an ovation was an inferior triumph accorded to victors in minor wars or unimportant battle. Its character and limitations, like those of the triumph, were strictly defined by law and custom. An enthusiastic demonstration in honor of an American civilian is nothing like that, and should not be called by its name.

Over for *About, In,* or *Concerning*. "Don't cry over spilt milk." "He rejoiced over his acquittal."

Over for *More than*. "A sum of over ten thousand dollars." "Upward of ten thousand dollars" is equally objectionable.

Over for *On*. "The policeman struck him over the head." If the blow was over the head it did not hit him.

Over with. "Let us have it over with." Omit with. A better expression is, Let us get done with it.

Outside of. Omit the preposition.

*

Pair for *Pairs*. If a word has a good plural use each form in its place.

Pants for *Trousers*. Abbreviated from pantaloons, which are no longer worn. Vulgar exceedingly.

Partially for *Partly.* A dictionary word, to swell the book.

Party for *Person.* "A party named Brown." The word, used in that sense, has the excuse that it is a word. Otherwise it is no better than "pants" and "gent." A person making an agreement, however, is a party to that agreement.

Patron for *Customer.*

Pay for *Give, Make,* etc. "He pays attention." "She paid a visit to Niagara." It is conceivable that one may owe attention or a visit to another person, but one cannot be indebted to a place.

Pay. "Laziness does not pay." "It does not pay to be uncivil." This use of the word is grossly commercial. Say, Indolence is unprofitable. There is no advantage in incivility.

Peek for *Peep.* Seldom heard in England, though common here. "I peeked out through the curtain and saw him." That it is a variant of peep is seen in the child's word peek-a-boo, equivalent to bo-peep. Better use the senior word.

Peculiar for *Odd,* or *Unusual.* Also sometimes used to denote distinction, or particularity. Properly a thing is peculiar only to another thing, of which it is characteristic, nothing else having it; as knowledge of the use of fire is peculiar to Man.

People for *Persons*. "Three people were killed." "Many people are superstitious." People has retained its parity of meaning with the Latin *populus*, whence it comes, and the word is not properly used except to designate a population, or large fractions of it considered in the mass. To speak of any stated or small number of persons as people is incorrect.

Per. "Five dollars *per* day." "Three *per* hundred." Say, three dollars a day; three in a hundred. If you must use the Latin preposition use the Latin noun too: *per diem; per centum*.

Perpetually for *Continually*. "The child is perpetually asking questions." What is done perpetually is done continually and forever.

Phenomenal for *Extraordinary*, or *Surprising*. Everything that occurs is phenomenal, for all that we know about is phenomena, appearances. Of realities, noumena, we are ignorant.

Plead (pronounced "pled") for *Pleaded*. "He plead guilty."

Plenty for *Plentiful*. "Fish and fowl were plenty."

Poetess. A foolish word, like "authoress."

Poetry for *Verse*. Not all verse is poetry; not all poetry is verse. Few persons can know, or hope to know, the one from the other, but he who has the humility to doubt (if such a one there be) should say verse if the composition is metrical.

Point Blank. "He fired at him point blank." This usually is intended to mean directly, or at short range. But point blank means the point at which the line of sight is crossed downward by the trajectory—the curve described by the missile.

Poisonous for *Venomous*. Hemlock is poisonous, but a rattlesnake is venomous.

Politics. The word is not plural because it happens to end with s.

Possess for *Have*. "To possess knowledge is to possess power." Possess is lacking in naturalness and unduly emphasizes the concept of ownership.

Practically for *Virtually*. This error is very common. "It is practically conceded." "The decision was practically unanimous." "The panther and the cougar are practically the same animal." These and similar misapplications of the word are virtually without excuse.

Predicate for *Found*, or *Base*. "I predicate my argument on universal experience." What is predicated of something is affirmed as an attribute of it, as omnipotence is predicated of the Deity.

Prejudice for *Prepossession*. Literally, a prejudice is merely a prejudgment—a decision before evidence—and may be favorable or unfavorable, but it is so much more frequently used in the latter sense than in the former that clarity is better got by the other word for reasonless approval.

Preparedness for *Readiness*. An awkward and needless word much used in discussion of national armaments, as, "Our preparedness for war."

Preside. "Professor Swackenhauer presided at the piano." "The deviled crab table was presided over by Mrs. Dooley." How would this sound? "The ginger pop stand was under the administration of President Woolwit, and Professor Sooffle presided at the flute."

Pretend for *Profess*. "I do not pretend to be infallible." Of course not; one does not care to confess oneself a pretender. To pretend is to try to deceive; one may profess quite honestly.

Preventative for *Preventive*. No such word as preventative.

Previous for *Previously*. "The man died previous to receipt of the letter."

Prior to for *Before*. Stilted.

Propose for *Purpose*, or *Intend*. "I propose to go to Europe." A mere intention is not a proposal.

Proposition for *Proposal*. "He made a proposition." In current slang almost anything is a proposition. A difficult enterprise is "a tough proposition," an agile wrestler, "a slippery proposition," and so forth.

Proportions for *Dimensions*. "A rock of vast proportions." Proportions relate to form; dimensions to magnitude.

Proven for *Proved*. Good Scotch, but bad English.

Proverbial for *Familiar*. "The proverbial dog in the manger." The animal is not "proverbial" for it is not mentioned in a proverb, but in a fable.

*

Quit for *Cease*, *Stop*. "Jones promises to quit drinking." In another sense, too, the word is commonly misused, as, "He has quit the town." Say, quitted.

Quite. "She is quite charming." If it is meant that she is entirely charming this is right, but usually the meaning intended to be conveyed is less than that—that she is rather, or somewhat, charming.

*

Raise for *Bring up, Grow, Breed,* etc. In this country a word-of-all-work: "raise children," "raise wheat," "raise cattle." Children are brought up, grain, hay and vegetables are grown, animals and poultry are bred.

Real for *Really,* or *Very.* "It is real good of him." "The weather was real cold."

Realize for *Conceive,* or *Comprehend.* "I could not realize the situation." Writers caring for precision use this word in the sense of to make real, not to make seem real. A dream seems real, but is actually realized when made to come true.

Recollect for *Remember.* To remember is to have in memory; to recollect is to recall what has escaped from memory. We remember automatically; in recollecting we make a conscious effort.

Redeem for *Retrieve.* "He redeemed his good name." Redemption (Latin *redemptio,* from *re* and *dimere*) is allied to ransom, and carries the sense of buying back; whereas to retrieve is merely to recover what was lost.

Redound for *Conduce*. "A man's honesty redounds to his advantage." We make a better use of the word if we say of one (for example) who has squandered a fortune, that its loss redounds to his advantage, for the word denotes a fluctuation, as from seeming evil to actual good; as villification may direct attention to one's excellent character.

Refused. "He was refused a crown." It is the crown that was refused to him. See *Given*.

Regular for *Natural*, or *Customary*. "Flattery of the people is the demagogue's regular means to political preferment." Regular properly relates to a rule (*regula*) more definite than the law of antecedent and consequent.

Reliable for *Trusty*, or *Trustworthy*. A word not yet admitted to the vocabulary of the fastidious, but with a strong backing for the place.

Remit for *Send*. "On receiving your bill I will remit the money." Remit does not mean that; it means give back, yield up, relinquish, etc. It means, also, to cancel, as in the phrase, the remission of sins.

Rendition for *Interpretation*, or *Performance*. "The actor's rendition of the part was good." Rendition means a surrender, or a giving back.

Reportorial. A vile word, improperly made. It assumes the Latinized spelling, "reportor." The Romans had not the word, for they were, fortunately for them, without the thing.

Repudiate for *Deny*. "He repudiated the accusation."

Reside for *Live*. "They reside in Hohokus." Stilted.

Residence for *Dwelling*, or *House*. See *Mansion*.

Respect for *Way*, or *Matter*. "They were alike in that respect." The misuse comes of abbreviating: the sentence properly written might be, They were alike in respect of that—i.e., with regard to that. The word in the bad sense has even been pluralized: "In many respects it is admirable."

Respective. "They went to their respective homes." The adjective here (if an adjective is thought necessary) should be several. In the adverbial form the word is properly used in the sentence following: John and James are bright and dull, respectively. That is, John is bright and James dull.

Responsible. "The bad weather is responsible for much sickness." "His intemperance was responsible for his crime." Responsibility is not an attribute of anything but human beings, and few of these can respond, in damages or otherwise. Responsible is nearly synonymous with accountable and answerable, which, also, are frequently misused.

Restive for *Restless.* These words have directly contrary meanings; the dictionaries' disallowance of their identity would be something to be thankful for, but that is a dream.

Retire for *Go to Bed.* English of the "genteel" sort. See *Genteel.*

Rev. for *The Rev.* "Rev. Dr. Smith."

Reverence for *Revere.*

Ride for *Drive.* On horseback one does drive, and in a vehicle one does ride, but a distinction is needed here, as in England; so, here as there, we may profitably make it, riding in the saddle and driving in the carriage.

Roomer for *Lodger.* See *Bedder* and *Mealer*—if you can find them.

Round for *About.* "They stood round." See *Around.*

Ruination for *Ruin.* Questionably derived and problematically needful.

Run for *Manage,* or *Conduct.* Vulgar—hardly better than slang.

*

Say for *Voice.* "He had no say in determining the matter." Vulgar.

Scholar for *Student,* or *Pupil.* A scholar is a person who is learned, not a person who is learning.

Score for *Win, Obtain,* etc. "He scored an advantage over his opponent." To score is not to win a point, but to record it.

Second-handed for *Second-hand.* There is no such word.

Secure for *Procure.* "He secured a position as book-keeper." "The dwarf secured a stick and guarded the jewels that he had found." Then it was the jewels that were secured.

Seldom ever. A most absurd locution.

Self-confessed. "A self-confessed assassin." Self is superfluous: one's sins cannot be confessed by another.

Sensation for *Emotion*. "The play caused a great sensation." "A sensational newspaper." A sensation is a physical feeling; an emotion, a mental. Doubtless the one usually accompanies the other, but the good writer will name the one that he has in mind, not the other. There are few errors more common than the one here noted.

Sense for *Smell*. "She sensed the fragrance of roses." Society English.

Set for *Sit*. "A setting hen."

Settee for *Settle*. This word belongs to the peasantry of speech.

Settle for *Pay*. "Settle the bill." "I shall take it now and settle for it later."

Shades for *Shade*. "Shades of Noah! how it rained!" "O shades of Caesar!" A shade is a departed soul, as conceived by the ancients; one to each mortal part is the proper allowance.

Show for *Chance*, or *Opportunity*. "He didn't stand a show." Say, He had no chance.

Sick for *Ill*. Good usage now limits this word to cases of nausea, but it is still legitimate in sickly, sickness, love-sick, and the like.

Side for *Agree*, or *Stand*. "I side with the Democrats." "He always sided with what he thought right."

Sideburns for *Burnsides*. A form of whiskers named from a noted general of the civil war, Ambrose E. Burnside. It seems to be thought that the word side has something to do with it, and that as an adjective it should come first, according to our idiom.

Side-hill for *Hillside*. A reasonless transposition for which it is impossible to assign a cause, unless it is abbreviated from side o' the hill.

Sideways for *Sidewise*. See *Endways*.

Since for *Ago*. "He came here not long since and died."

Smart for *Bright*, or *Able*. An Americanism that is dying out. But "smart" has recently come into use for fashionable, which is almost as bad.

Snap for *Period* (of time) or *Spell*. "A cold snap." This is a word of incomprehensible origin in that sense; we can know only that its parents were not respectable. "Spell" is itself not very well-born.

So—as. See *As—as*.

So for *True*. "If you see it in the Daily Livercomplaint it is so." "Is that so?" Colloquial and worse.

Solemnize. This word rightly means to make solemn, not to perform, or celebrate, ceremoniously something already solemn, as a marriage, or a mass. We have no exact synonym, but this explains, rather than justifies, its use.

Some for *Somewhat.* "He was hurt some."

Soon for *Willingly.* "I would as soon go as stay." "That soldier would sooner eat than fight." Say, rather eat.

Space for *Period.* "A long space of time." Space is so different a thing from time that the two do not go well together.

Spend for *Pass.* "We shall spend the summer in Europe." Spend denotes a voluntary relinquishment, but time goes from us against our will.

Square for *Block.* "He lives three squares away." A city block is seldom square.

Squirt for *Spurt.* Absurd.

Stand and *Stand for* for *Endure.* "The patient stands pain well." "He would not stand for misrepresentation."

Standpoint for *Point of View*, or *Viewpoint.*

State for *Say*. "He stated that he came from Chicago." "It is stated that the president is angry." We state a proposition, or a principle, but say that we are well. And we say our prayers—some of us.

Still Continue. "The rain still continues." Omit still; it is contained in the other word.

Stock. "I take no stock in it." Disagreeably commercial. Say, I have no faith in it. Many such metaphorical expressions were unobjectionable, even pleasing, in the mouth of him who first used them, but by constant repetition by others have become mere slang, with all the offensiveness of plagiarism. The prime objectionableness of slang is its hideous lack of originality. Until mouth-worn it is not slang.

Stop for *Stay*. "Prayer will not stop the ravages of cholera." Stop is frequently misused for stay in another sense of the latter word: "He is stopping at the hotel." Stopping is not a continuing act; one cannot be stopping who has already stopped.

Stunt. A word recently introduced and now overworked, meaning a task, or performance in one's trade, or calling,—doubtless a variant of stint, without that word's suggestion of allotment and limitation. It is still in the reptilian stage of evolution.

Subsequent for *Later*, or *Succeeding*. Legitimate enough, but ugly and needless. "He was subsequently hanged." Say, afterward.

Substantiate for *Prove*. Why?

Success. "The project was a success." Say, was successful. Success should not have the indefinite article.

Such Another for *Another Such*. There is illustrious authority for this—in poetry. Poets are a lawless folk, and may do as they please so long as they do please.

Such for *So*. "He had such weak legs that he could not stand." The absurdity of this is made obvious by changing the form of the statement: "His legs were such weak that he could not stand." If the word is an adverb in the one sentence it is in the other. "He is such a great bore that none can endure him." Say, so great a bore.

Suicide. This is never a verb. "He suicided." Say, He killed himself, or He took his own life. See *Commit Suicide*.

Supererogation. To supererogate is to overpay, or to do more than duty requires. But the excess must be in the line of duty; merely needless and irrelevant action is not supererogation. The word is not a natural one, at best.

Sure for *Surely*. "They will come, sure." Slang.

Survive for *Live*, or *Persist*. Survival is an outliving, or outlasting of something else. "The custom survives" is wrong, but a custom may survive its utility. Survive is a transitive verb.

Sustain for *Incur*. "He sustained an injury." "He sustained a broken neck." That means that although his neck was broken he did not yield to the mischance.

*

Talented for *Gifted*. These are both past participles, but there was once the verb to gift, whereas there was never the verb "to talent." If Nature did not talent a person the person is not talented.

Tantamount for *Equivalent*. "Apology is tantamount to confession." Let this ugly word alone; it is not only illegitimate, but ludicrously suggests catamount.

Tasty for *Tasteful*. Vulgar.

Tear Down for *Pull Down.* "The house was torn down." This is an indigenous solecism; they do not say so in England.

Than Whom. See *Whom.*

The. A little word that is terribly overworked. It is needlessly affixed to names of most diseases: "the cholera," "the smallpox," "the scarlet fever," and such. Some escape it: we do not say, "the sciatica," nor "the locomotor ataxia." It is too common in general propositions, as, "The payment of interest is the payment of debt." "The virtues that are automatic are the best." "The tendency to falsehood should be checked." "Kings are not under the control of the law." It is impossible to note here all forms of this misuse, but a page of almost any book will supply abundant instance. We do not suffer so abject slavery to the definite article as the French, but neither do we manifest their spirit of rebellion by sometimes cutting off the oppressor's tail. One envies the Romans, who had no article, definite or indefinite.

The Following. "Washington wrote the following." The following what? Put in the noun. "The following animals are ruminants." It is not the animals that follow, but their names.

The Same. "They cooked the flesh of the lion and ate the same." "An old man lived in a cave, and the same was a cripple." In humorous composition this may do, though it is not funny; but in serious work use the regular pronoun.

Then as an Adjective. "The then governor of the colony." Say, the governor of the colony at that time.

Those Kind for *That Kind.* "Those kind of things." Almost too absurd for condemnation, and happily not very common out of the class of analphabets.

Though for *If.* "She wept as though her heart was broken." Many good writers, even some devoid of the lexicographers' passion for inclusion and approval, have specifically defended this locution, backing their example by their precept. Perhaps it is a question of taste; let us attend their cry and pass on.

Thrifty for *Thriving.* "A thrifty village." To thrive is an end; thrift is a means to that end.

Through for *Done.* "The lecturer is through talking." "I am through with it." Say, I have done with it.

To. As part of an infinitive it should not be separated from the other part by an adverb, as, "to hastily think," for hastily to think, or, to think hastily. Condemnation of the split infinitive is now pretty general, but it is only recently that any one seems to have thought of it. Our forefathers and we elder writers of this generation used it freely and without shame—perhaps because it had not a name, and our crime could not be pointed out without too much explanation.

To for *At.* "We have been to church," "I was to the theater." One can go to a place, but one cannot be to it.

Total. "The figures totaled 10,000." Say, The total of the figures was 10,000.

Transaction for *Action*, or *Incident.* "The policeman struck the man with his club, but the transaction was not reported." "The picking of a pocket is a criminal transaction." In a transaction two or more persons must have an active or assenting part; as, a business transaction, Transactions of the Geographical Society, etc. The Society's action would be better called Proceedings.

Transpire for *Occur, Happen*, etc. "This event transpired in 1906." Transpire (*trans*, through, and *spirare*, to breathe) means leak out, that is, become known. What transpired in 1906 may have occurred long before.

Trifling for *Trivial*. "A trifling defect"; "a trifling error."

Trust for *Wealthy Corporation*. There are few trusts; capitalists have mostly abandoned the trust form of combination.

Try an Experiment. An experiment is a trial; we cannot try a trial. Say, make.

Try and for *Try to*. "I will try and see him." This plainly says that my effort to see him will succeed—which I cannot know and do not wish to affirm. "Please try and come." This colloquial slovenliness of speech is almost universal in this country, but freedom of speech is one of our most precious possessions.

*

Ugly for *Ill-natured, Quarrelsome*. What is ugly is the temper, or disposition, not the person having it.

Under-handed and *Under-handedly* for *Under-hand*. See *Off-handed*.

Unique. "This is very unique." "The most unique house in the city." There are no degrees of uniqueness: a thing is unique if there is not another like it. The word has nothing to do with oddity, strangeness, nor picturesqueness.

United States as a Singular Noun. "The United States is for peace." The fact that we are in some ways one nation has nothing to do with it; it is enough to know that the word States is plural—if not, what is State? It would be pretty hard on a foreigner skilled in the English tongue if he could not venture to use our national name without having made a study of the history of our Constitution and political institutions. Grammar has not a speaking acquaintance with politics, and patriotic pride is not schoolmaster to syntax.

Unkempt for *Disordered, Untidy,* etc. Unkempt means uncombed, and can properly be said of nothing but the hair.

Use for *Treat.* "The inmates were badly used." "They use him harshly."

Utter for *Absolute, Entire,* etc. Utter has a damnatory signification and is to be used of evil things only. It is correct to say utter misery, but not "utter happiness"; utterly bad, but not "utterly good."

*

Various for *Several.* "Various kinds of men." Kinds are various of course, for they vary—that is what makes them kinds. Use various only when, in speaking of a number of things, you wish to direct attention to their variety—their difference, one from another. "The dividend was distributed among the various stockholders." The stockholders vary, as do all persons, but that is irrelevant and was not in mind. "Various persons have spoken to me of you." Their variation is unimportant; what is meant is that there was a small indefinite number of them; that is, several.

Ventilate for *Express, Disclose*, etc. "The statesman ventilated his views." A disagreeable and dog-eared figure of speech.

Verbal for *Oral.* All language is verbal, whether spoken or written, but audible speech is oral. "He did not write, but communicated his wishes verbally." It would have been a verbal communication, also, if written.

Vest for *Waistcoat.* This is American, but as all Americans are not in agreement about it it is better to use the English word.

Vicinity for *Vicinage*, or *Neighborhood.* "He lives in this vicinity." If neither of the other words is desired say, He lives in the vicinity of this place, or, better, He lives near by.

View of. "He invested with the view of immediate profit." "He enlisted with the view of promotion." Say, with a view to.

Vulgar for *Immodest, Indecent.* It is from *vulgus*, the common people, the mob, and means both common and unrefined, but has no relation to indecency.

*

Way for *Away.* "Way out at sea." "Way down South."

Ways for *Way.* "A squirrel ran a little ways along the road." "The ship looked a long ways off." This surprising word calls loudly for depluralization.

Wed for *Wedded.* "They were wed at noon." "He wed her in Boston." The word wed in all its forms as a substitute for marry, is pretty hard to bear.

Well. As a mere meaningless prelude to a sentence this word is overtasked. "Well, I don't know about that." "Well, you may try." "Well, have your own way."

Wet for *Wetted.* See *Bet.*

Where for *When.* "Where there is reason to expect criticism write discreetly."

Which for *That.* "The boat which I engaged had a hole in it." But a parenthetical clause may rightly be introduced by which; as, The boat, which had a hole in it, I nevertheless engaged. Which and that are seldom interchangeable; when they are, use that. It sounds better.

Whip for *Chastise,* or *Defeat.* To whip is to beat with a whip. It means nothing else.

Whiskers for *Beard.* The whisker is that part of the beard that grows on the cheek. See *Chin Whiskers.*

Who for *Whom.* "Who do you take me for?"

Whom for *Who.* "The man whom they thought was dead is living." Here the needless introduction of was entails the alteration of whom to who. "Remember whom it is that you speak of." "George Washington, than whom there was no greater man, loved a jest." The misuse of whom after than is almost universal. Who and whom trip up many a good writer, although, unlike which and who, they require nothing but knowledge of grammar.

Widow Woman. Omit woman.

Will and *Shall.* Proficiency in the use of these apparently troublesome words must be sought in text-books on grammar and rhetoric, where the subject will be found treated with a more particular attention, and at greater length, than is possible in a book of the character of this. Briefly and generally, in the first person, a mere intention is indicated by shall, as, I shall go; whereas will denotes some degree of compliance or determination, as, I will go—as if my going had been requested or forbidden. In the second and the third person, will merely forecasts, as, You (or he) will go; but shall implies something of promise, permission or compulsion by the speaker, as, You (or he) shall go. Another and less obvious compulsion—that of circumstance—speaks in shall, as sometimes used with good effect: In Germany you shall not turn over a chip without uncovering a philosopher. The sentence is barely more than indicative, shall being almost, but not quite, equivalent to can.

Win out. Like its antithesis, "lose out," this reasonless phrase is of sport, "sporty."

Win for *Won.* "I went to the race and win ten dollars." This atrocious solecism seems to be unknown outside the world of sport, where may it ever remain.

Without for *Unless.* "I cannot go without I recover." Peasantese.

Witness for *See.* To witness is more than merely to see, or observe; it is to observe, and to tell afterward.

Would-be. "The would-be assassin was arrested." The word doubtless supplies a want, but we can better endure the want than the word. In the instance of the assassin, it is needless, for he who attempts to murder is an assassin, whether he succeeds or not.

*